BEYOND THE BATTLEFIELD

Homefront Heroes

ALLEN R. WELLS

Rourke
Educational Media

A Division of
Carson
Dellosa
Education.

T0011541

Before Reading: *Building Background Knowledge and Vocabulary*

Building background knowledge can help children process new information and build upon what they already know. Before reading a book, it is important to tap into what children already know about the topic. This will help them develop their vocabulary and increase their reading comprehension.

Questions and Activities to Build Background Knowledge:

1. Look at the front cover of the book and read the title. What do you think this book will be about?
2. What do you already know about this topic?
3. Take a book walk and skim the pages. Look at the table of contents, photographs, captions, and bold words. Did these text features give you any information or predictions about what you will read in this book?

Vocabulary: *Vocabulary Is Key to Reading Comprehension*

Use the following directions to prompt a conversation about each word.

- Read the vocabulary words.
- What comes to mind when you see each word?
- What do you think each word means?

Vocabulary Words:

- civilian
- drafted
- ghetto
- propaganda
- rationing
- volunteers

During Reading: *Reading for Meaning and Understanding*

To achieve deep comprehension of a book, children are encouraged to use close reading strategies. During reading, it is important to have children stop and make connections. These connections result in deeper analysis and understanding of a book.

Close Reading a Text

During reading, have children stop and talk about the following:

- Any confusing parts
- Any unknown words
- Text to text, text to self, text to world connections
- The main idea in each chapter or heading

Encourage children to use context clues to determine the meaning of any unknown words. These strategies will help children learn to analyze the text more thoroughly as they read.

When you are finished reading this book, turn to the next-to-last page for **After-Reading Questions** and an **Activity**.

Table of Contents

Groups Help the Homefront....................4

Civilian Heroes...............................20

Memory Game.................................30

Index......................................31

After-Reading Questions.....................31

Activity 31

About the Author 32

GROUPS HELP THE HOMEFRONT

Girl Guides

During World War II, millions of men and women left their jobs to join the war effort. Many of them were teachers, electricians, nurses, and mechanics. Who would fill in for these essential workers at home? In the United Kingdom (UK), the Girl Guides stepped up.

The Girl Guide Association was created in 1912 after a group of girls in the UK showed up at a Boy Scout rally calling themselves Girl Scouts. The organization grew rapidly. By the time World War II started in 1939, there were 750,000 Guides in the UK.

A group of Guides wave to an air ambulance donated to the war effort in their name by Mary, the Princess Royal.

Jeanne Day was just one of the many who left their jobs at home to volunteer for the war effort.

During WWII, Guides worked to fill the positions the country needed. They started learning how to perform first aid, electrical work, and mechanical work. They took the place of teachers and nurses in childcare.

Guides also helped create spaces for those who had to evacuate their homes because of the war. They cleaned out empty houses and turned churches into childcare centers. They got creative and used whatever was available to them.

The future queen of England practices her first aid on her sister, Princess Margaret.

The UK government noticed how helpful the Guides were as **volunteers**. They decided to ask the Guides to give the public wartime cooking lessons. Guides gave lessons on "Blitz" cooking. Blitz cooking was cooking with an oven created out of the bricks you might find in rubble if buildings in an area had been bombed.

During the war, the government controlled the public's food supply to make sure there weren't food shortages.

The aftermath of a bombing in London, England.

volunteers (vah-luhn-TEERZ): people who do a job without pay

This would mean people sometimes had limited meals they could cook. Guides also came up with creative recipes to share with the public. One recipe was a mock fishcake that was actually made using potatoes and anchovy sauce.

Ration books like this one were given out by the government. They listed the foods a person was allowed to buy.

Girl Scouts

In the United States, a similar girls' organization got to work during WWII. The Girl Scouts also wanted to make a difference from the home front. They held drives to gather things like scrap metal, rubber, and cloth. These materials were all donated to help the war effort.

Rather than selling cookies during the war, the Girl Scouts sold war bonds. When someone bought a war bond, the government would use the money that went toward purchasing the bond for the war effort. Ten years after the war bond was purchased, it could be cashed in and the government would return the money to the person who bought the bond.

Half the Metal in
every ship
every tank
every gun
is SCRAP!
THROW *YOUR* SCRAP
INTO THE FIGHT!

A group of Girl Scouts with
First Lady Eleanor Roosevelt.

The metal that was collected at scrap
metal drives would be used to make
airplanes, ships, and other equipment.

A war bond from WWII

The Girl Scouts also acted as bike messengers and delivered mail. They taught defense classes for women. They taught survival skills and showed how to comfort children during air raids. If they saw a need in their community that they could fill, that's what they did!

Troops in Camps

In WWII, Japan and the U.S. were enemies. Doubting their loyalty to the war effort, the U.S. forced Japanese Americans into internment camps. The U.S. didn't need any reason other than Japanese heritage to force these American citizens to leave their homes. In these inhumane camps, girls got together and formed official Girl Scout troops, though not much is known about these troops. In 1998, the U.S. Congress apologized for the camps and paid $20,000 to any surviving victims as a symbol of the wrong they suffered.

Victory Gardens

World War I created food shortages across Europe. Farmers were **drafted** into the military and their fields were left unattended. Many farms in Europe were destroyed when they became battlefields.

When the U.S. got involved in WWI in 1917, President Woodrow Wilson encouraged Americans to plant and grow their own vegetable gardens. This would not only allow the U.S. to ship more food to Europe, but it would also help prevent food shortages at home. These gardens were called "war gardens" for most of WWI and "victory gardens" at the end of the war and beyond.

drafted (draft-id): ordered to join the armed forces

President Woodrow Wilson

A man tends to his victory garden during WWI.

The war garden movement became incredibly popular. The idea spread with the help of **propaganda** posters and by word of mouth.

Americans planted 3 million new gardens in 1917. They dug plots in creative ways. They turned their own yards, school grounds, company grounds, public parks, and even vacant lots into vegetable gardens. Children were encouraged to participate. The Bureau of Education called children "soldiers of the soil." At the end of WWI, an estimated 1.45 million quarts of canned fruits and vegetables were produced from these gardens.

propaganda (prah-puh-GAN-duh): information that is spread to influence the way people think, to gain supporters, or to damage an opposing group. It is often biased information, but it is not always negative

Many propaganda posters were created to spread the victory garden movement.

Victory gardens were used again during WWII. In 1943, First Lady Eleanor Roosevelt led by example and planted a victory garden on the front lawn of the White House. WWII brought food **rationing** to the U.S., but if someone had a garden, they could grow extra food for themselves and others. People used flower boxes, rooftops, and any extra spot of land they could find to grow vegetables.

By the end of WWII, there were an estimated 20 million victory gardens. These gardens helped with food shortages, boosted morale, and allowed those who weren't directly involved in the war to help out.

rationing (RASH-uhn-ing): allowing each person to have a fixed amount of something, especially food

Victory gardens were planted wherever the space was available, including in the middle of big cities.

CIVILIAN HEROES

Edith Cavell

Edith Cavell was a British **civilian** who worked as a nurse in Brussels, Belgium, during WWI. She was visiting her mother in Norfolk, England, when the war began. Cavell knew her nursing skills would be needed. Even though Belgium was occupied by the German forces, she felt it was her duty to return.

civilian (suh-VIL-yuhn): a person who is not a member of the armed forces

Edith Cavell

Cavell's hospital in Belgium was turned into a Red Cross Hospital where those who were injured in the war were sent. Cavell worked to help the wounded, both Belgian people and German troops.

The hospital also cared for British and French Allied soldiers. They were patients at the hospital, but as enemies of the Germans, they were also prisoners. Cavell decided to help them escape the hospital and Belgium altogether. She worked with a secret network to get these soldiers money and fake identification cards that would help them escape across the Dutch border.

Allies in the War

The two sides during WWI were the Allies and the Central Powers. The Allies were made up of Russia, France, Great Britain, Italy, Romania, Japan, and the United States. The Central Powers were made up of Germany, Austria-Hungary, Bulgaria, and the Ottoman Empire.

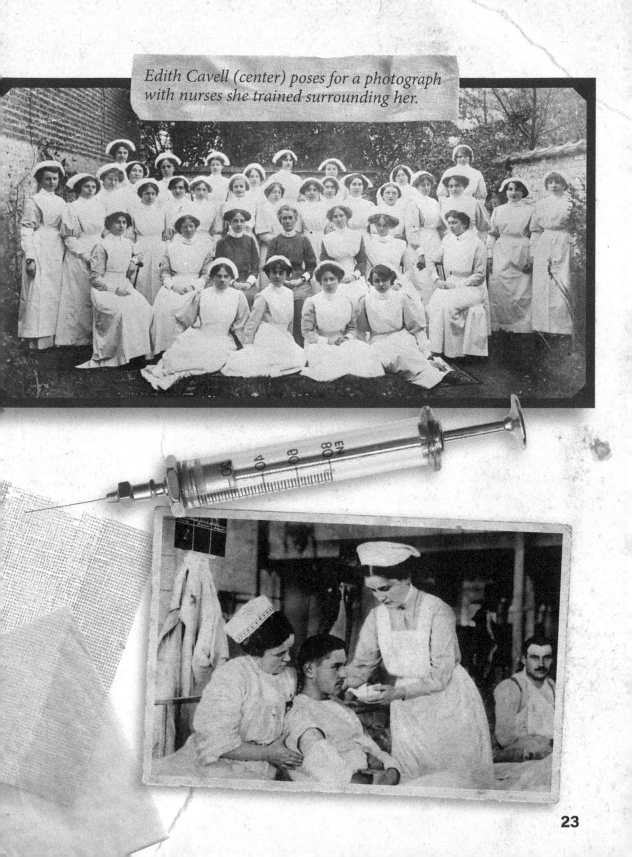

Edith Cavell (center) poses for a photograph with nurses she trained surrounding her.

In August 1915, a former French soldier working as a German spy found the secret escape tunnel under the hospital. The authorities then discovered that prisoners were being smuggled out. Cavell was arrested shortly after the discovery.

Cavell was given a trial where she confessed to everything. She was found guilty and sentenced to death. Politicians and people around the world cried out for her release, but to no avail. Cavell was executed on October 12, 1915. Cavell is remembered as a hero who saved many lives while sacrificing her own.

A memorial to Cavell stands in London, England.

MURDERED

OCTOBER 12TH, 1915

By THE Huns

MISS EDITH CAVELL

ENLIST IN THE 99th

AND HEL

Anti-German propaganda was created after Cavell was executed.

MISS EDITH CAVELL
MURDERED
October 12th 1915

REMEMBER!

Irena Sendler

When WWII began, Irena Sendler was a young Polish social worker in Warsaw, Poland. When Nazi Germany invaded Poland, they crammed the Jewish population of Warsaw into one small, closed off, and guarded section of the city. It was called the **ghetto**. Sendler had to do something. She got involved with an underground organization to save Jewish people called *Zegota*. Her focus was on rescuing children.

ghetto (GET-oh): a section of a city that was set apart and in which Jews were forced to live

Since Sendler was a social worker, she had special permission to get into the ghetto. While she was there, she spoke with parents. She tried to convince them to let her attempt to rescue their children.

Irena Sendler

Children gather together in the Warsaw ghetto.

If parents agreed, there were a few ways Sendler got the children out of the city to safety. Some were transported in coffins. Others were moved in potato sacks. And still others were hidden in the floorboards of ambulances. Ultimately, they were all sent to a church where they would receive new names and identities. Then they were sent to an orphanage or placed with a non-Jewish family, safe from the Nazis.

By the end of WWII, Sendler managed to send around 2,500 Jewish children to safety.

This photograph shows some of the children Sendler rescued from the Warsaw ghetto.

Sendler survived the war and went on to be nominated for the Nobel Peace Prize.

Memory Game

Look at the pictures. What do you remember reading on the pages where each image appeared?

 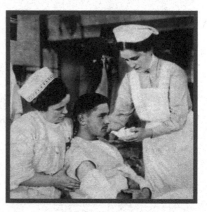

Index

Allies 22

Belgium 20, 22

Central Powers 22

Eleanor Roosevelt 11, 18

internment camp 12

Poland 26

World War I (WWI) 14, 15, 16,
   20, 22

World War II (WWII) 4, 6, 10, 11,
   12, 18, 26, 28

After-Reading Questions

1. What was one thing the Girl Guides did during WWII?

2. What are some reasons someone might start a victory garden?

3. What were internment camps?

4. How did Edith Cavell assist in the war effort during WWI?

5. How did Irena Sendler help the Jewish people during WWII?

Activity

These homefront heroes put their beliefs in action in order to create change. Think about groups you have heard about that fight for change or try to correct injustice. Choose one cause and brainstorm a list of things you might be able to do to help.

About the Author

Allen R. Wells loved researching and refamiliarizing himself with the hidden figures in this book. Allen admires their perseverance and determination to fight for what they believe. He writes wherever he finds inspiration. He lives in Atlanta, Georgia, where he works as a mechanical engineer and children's author.

www.rourkeeducationalmedia.com

PHOTO CREDITS: cover: eastern archive/ Shutterstock.com, LiliGraphie/ Shutterstock.com, Lebazele/ Getty Images, images and videos/ Shutterstock.com, FabrikaSimf/ Shutterstock.com; Inside Cover: DarkBird/ Shutterstock.com, Lebazele/ Getty Images; TOC: waku/ Shutterstock.com; TOC, page 32: TADDEUS/ Shutterstock.com; page 4, 10, 14, 20, 26: DarkBird/ Shutterstock.com; page 4-5: Here/ Shutterstock.com; page 5: Lebazele/ Getty Images, photo provided by the family of Jeanne Day, Nataliia K/ Shutterstock.com; page 5, 7, 8, 9, 11, 15, 17, 19, 21, 23, 24, 25, 27, 29: Picsfive/ Shutterstock.com; page 5, 30: Associated Press; page 6: Peyker/ Shutterstock.com; page 7: Associated Press, Nataliia K/ Shutterstock.com; page: 6-7, 14-15, 22-23 24-25, 30-31: DarkBird/ Shutterstock.com; page 6-7: images and videos/ Shutterstock.com; page 8: Everett Collection/ Shutterstock.com, DarkBird/ Shutterstock.com; page 9: chrisdorney/ Shutterstock.com, Red pepper/ Shutterstock.com, dlerick/ Getty Images; page 10-11, 20-21, 26-27: DarkBird/ Shutterstock.com; page 11: National Archives and Records Administration, Library of Congress, Prints & Photographs Division, photograph by Harris & Ewing, [reproduction number, e.g., LC-USZ62-123456]; page 11, 30: Library of Congress; page 12-13: sozon/ Shutterstock.com; page 12: National Archives and Records Administration; page 12, 22: LiliGraphie/ Shutterstock.com; page 13: Library of Congress, Prints & Photographs Division, photograph by Harris & Ewing, [reproduction number, e.g., LC-USZ62-123456], Library of Congress, Prints & Photographs Division, FSA/OWI Collection, [reproduction number, e.g., LC-USF34-9058-C], Kristina Kristamore/ Shutterstock.com; page 15: Everett Collection/ Shutterstock.com, Library of Congress, Prints & Photographs Division, photograph by Harris & Ewing, [reproduction number, e.g., LC-USZ62-123456], Diana Taliun/ Shutterstock.com; page 16-17, 28-29, photonova/ Shutterstock.com; page 17: Food and Drug Administration, Library of Congress, Prints & Photographs Division, [reproduction number, e.g., LC-DIG-ppmsca-12345]; page 18-19: George Marks/ Getty Images, Tolga TEZCAN/ Getty Iamges, Olga_Z/ Getty Images; page 19: Yudhistira99/ Shutterstock.com, Jiri Hera/ Shutterstock.com; page 19, 30: The U.S. National Archives/ Flickr; page 21: DarkBird/ Shutterstock.com; page 21, 30: Photos.com/ Getty Images; page 23: German Red Cross, DarkBird/ Shutterstock.com, revers/ Shutterstock.com, Imperial War Museum; page 23-24: Walter Cicchetti/Shutterstock.com; page 24: Ron Ellis/ Shutterstock.com; page 25: IWM Art.IWM PST 12217, Canadian War Museum; page 27: Wikimedia Commons, Olena Zaskochenko/ Shutterstock.com, Wikimedia Commons, Vitaly Korovin/ Shutterstock.com, adolf martinez soler/ Shutterstock.com; page 28: Wikimedia Commons, DarkBird/ Shutterstock.com; page 29: KATARINA STOLTZ/REUTERS/Newscom, World History Archive/Newscom, DarkBird/Shutterstock.com, Paramonov Alexander/Shutterstock.com, andersphoto/Shutterstock.com

Edited by: Hailey Scragg
Cover and interior design by: Morgan Burnside

Library of Congress PCN Data

Homefront Heroes / Allen R. Wells
 (Beyond the Battlefield)
  ISBN 978-1-73164-902-7 (hard cover)
  ISBN 978-1-73164-850-1 (soft cover)
  ISBN 978-1-73164-954-6 (e-Book)
  ISBN 978-1-73165-006-1 (ePub)
Library of Congress Control Number: 2021935270

Rourke Educational Media
Printed in the United States of America
02-09422119570

CPSIA information can be obtained
at www.ICGtesting.com
Printed in the USA
JSHW020239020422
24508JS00002B/11